Under the Radar

POEMS

Under the Radar

SOME RHYME . . .
SOME REASON/SOME RANT . . .
SOME RAVE

by

S. A. GERBER

iUniverse, Inc.
Bloomington

Under the Radar
Some Rhyme . . . Some Reason/Some Rant . . . Some Rave

iUniverse books may be ordered through booksellers or by contacting:

iUniverse
1663 Liberty Drive
Bloomington, IN 47403
www.iuniverse.com
1-800-Authors (1-800-288-4677)

ISBN: 978-1-4759-2475-6 (sc)
ISBN: 978-1-4759-2476-3 (ebk)

Printed in the United States of America

iUniverse rev. date: 05/25/2012

"Poets utter great and wise things which they do not themselves understand."

—Plato

"If I don't write to empty my mind, I go mad."

—Lord Byron

"How vain it is to sit down and write when you have not stood up to live."

—Henry David Thoreau

"The only thing that can save the world is the reclaiming of the awareness of the world. That's what poetry does."

—Allen Ginsberg

"Poetry is life distilled."

—Gwendolyn Brooks

"Publishing a volume of verse is like dropping a rose petal down the Grand Canyon and waiting for the echo."

—Don Marquis

For the two
Mrs. Gerbers

Contents

* *We Are*-Published in Blue Collar Review-Winter 2011-2012.
* *Elemental Aggression*-Published in Desert Voices Magazine-Volume 8-May 2010.
* *Test*-Published in Blue Collar Review-Autumn 2009.

Foreword

by Michael Prescott

S. A. Gerber—Steven, my friend and fellow poet—has given me the honor and privilege of reading this collection of his poems and writing a foreword to it.

The title poem of *Under the Radar* shows Steven's poetic skills but also shows, in the poem's overly modest self-abasement, his underestimation of himself as a poet. Steven just does not realize how good a poet he truly is.

Despite the title, I believe this book should put S. A. Gerber, poet, *on* the radar, where I hope he is noticed by those who will keep him there.

I've been reading Steven's poems since he first began expressing his inner spirit in words of poetry and poetic prose. I knew right away that here was a true fellow poet whose heart, like Edgar Allan Poe's, is a lute and whose mind, like Jean-Paul Sartre's, resolves into *les mots*—the words.

As with many of the best poets, Steven pours into his poetry a wide range of human emotions. Let me give now some of my impressions of this, his first book of poetry offered to me and to you.

The very cheerful, life-embracing "New Day Sun" makes the reader feel—as opposed to Archibald MacLeish's "always rising of the night"—the equally real always rising of the next day's sun, fresh with new life and new possibilities.

The poem "Twelve in '66" gives a potpourri sampling of nostalgic tidbits from the 1960s. The work evokes the general ambiance of the 1960s with a fine representative selection. Those who remember that time as well as those who do not will enjoy this poem. Many aspects of that era have filtered into our collective memory, and Steven brings them back.

As to Steven's lute, he has an excellent artistry of language that often enhances his expression of feelings and thoughts. Often he brings fresh perspectives. For example, "Bleak Witness" breaks with the usual concept of light as good and dark as bad with these lines: "A harsh, burning light invades / the comforting darkness." Yes, at times darkness can be comforting, and light can be harsh. And who fears most the revealing glare of light? Listen to this gem of poetic diction and sound: "The guilty scatter like / oiled drops of mercury." This accurate simile also paints a crisp, clear image.

I highly recommend the poem "Dream State" because I fully feel the truth Steven writes in it. His phrase "My pen to / coffee-stained paper" fits my own life as a poet as well. Steven carries us to a place where "My precious time / is my own." A well-wrought ending—without giving it away—caps this poem.

Sometimes Steven sinks a deep drill into the depth of his subconscious, and out gushes the black gold of human yearnings. Deep, often inexpressible wishes burst with the force of repressed hunger and thirst into free-flying words seeking to carry those truths. The subconscious often wants things that are impossible either absolutely impossible in themselves or because contradictory, they cannot exist together.

"Literary Wish List" expresses the yearning to be "safe in the assumption / there will never be a challenger" at the same time as wanting "to soak up life" and yet also "go out like Hemingway, / with a blast, double-barreled." This poem shows the disparate chaos of contradictory desires out of which an artist must carve his or her final works.

By contrast, "Some Simple Wants" is all about throwing off rules and restrictions that divide the spiritual person from the physical person, thus encouraging full, free, simultaneous expression. This is another of the great, deep desires of our subconscious, but it also emerges as a quite conscious aspiration, and with effort it can be fulfilled in varying degrees. Steven ranges from political pieces—and he reminds us in his poetry that *p* is the first letter also of *poison*—to the ultimate concerns of philosophy and human fate. Thus, "My Country" manages to convey his love of his country simultaneously with his disappointments with liberals' abdication of their lofty goals of equal opportunity, job training, helping the hungry and the homeless have food and shelter, and various other needed social safety nets. However, some good is still being done, and not all needy people are allowed to sink without a life preserver. Steven saves his greatest outrage for those who would eliminate even this. He deplores the rise of fascist values replacing compassion and social justice.

This perspective is even more apparent in the stunning "We Are," something of a poetic manifesto—a call to arms of sorts and a dire warning. This piece draws that ever-broadening line separating the "haves and the have-nots" with vivid examples of historic suppression that came and continue to come from the misuse of power and wealth. Once again, Steven uses names, symbols, and events to evoke feelings, set a mood, and list most of those whom he considers "on the side of the angels" opposing the 1 percent.

He leaves the choice to the "ruling class," for now, in a wonderful analogy, saying that it could get "Altamont" (a violent concert at the end of the 1960s) or "Woodstock" (the festival for love and peace the same year) as an ultimate solution. At the same time he cautions the ruling class that it being its game now, "this, too, shall pass."

"Intrude" puts its finger on the ultimate question: Which side of life will eventually win out and leave the mark of its victory forever? Will it be the light—represented as the dawn—or will it be the dark side, putting humanity once again into a long, chilling night?

Steven is a prolific poet who has been pouring out his heart and mind in poetry form since 1999. He could easily assemble his many poems into a number of single-themed anthologies with many different themes. He probably will begin this in the future. But here, he offers us a selection representing, in one volume, his many different views, feelings, ideas, evaluations, fears, hopes, and dreams. The poems I have commented on show some of his range. I will now comment on just two more, which concern death and life.

Steven honors his father with the poignant "Wish You Were Here." An honorable veteran of World War II, Steven's father was there at D-Day and served in other key battles. A survivor of the war, Steven's father was killed by cancer at age sixty-six. The anguish of this injustice caused Steven to cry this truth: "War is hell . . . / so is life"—or so it seems that life can be. The sentiment that life is hell here means that life can be unjust—with loss and suffering. In this poem, Steven writes of his father, "My pop was there—3rd Armored / Division—Omaha Beach." He has pride in his dad's accomplishment.

Then the grief sets in: "He was there, / but he's not here." In the compact energy of these words, I feel his grief, just as I feel mine.

Lastly, I turn to Steven's great poem "Exchange." Imagine the exchange window of a department store, only this one is the great cosmic department store. Imagine exchanging your fifty-inch plasma screen television for a great library—a library like Steven's. Some people might not want that. Still, surely everyone would like to make this exchange: "All the politicians / for one honest plan." But it is the final exchange that Steven imagines that most moves my heart, that makes me weep with longing: "this life / for immortality."

I have been reading Steven Gerber's poetry since he began writing poems. He is a published poet already, with several successful magazine submissions. But here is something special. This is his first book of poetry to be published. You have an excellent writer's first book of poems in your hands, and it is ready for you to read and enjoy. Profit from the wisdom of life culled from a lifetime of diverse experiences, filtered through the spirit and mind of a skillful and sensitive poet.

I wish Steven Gerber all the success for this book that it deserves. I hope, too, he will publish many successful books of poetry in the future. He has been "under the radar" for too long.

—Michael Prescott (Michael LP)

Chronicle

I remember when might was right
during the insidious cold war spree.
There were unlocked doors by day or night,
and only black-and-white TV.
No remotes, phones with dials,
and nickel candy bars.
Roofs of wood, not of tiles,
and fins on big-ass cars.
Oswald shot on live TV,
and the Beatles Sunday night.
Playhouse 90, Pinky Lee,
and the Liston-Patterson fight.
Huddling beneath a schoolhouse desk,
warding off surprise attack.
'Dem Brooklyn bums who came out West,
Billie Holiday's death from smack.
Fanny Hill, Mickey Spillane,
and *Catcher in the Rye*.
Alger Hiss and Lois Lane,
and Nixon's desperate try.
Goldwater runs in '64,
advisers run Southeast Asia.
Birchers knocking at your door,
surf films and *Fantasia*.
A monk on fire in the street,
drawing final breath.
Miss America, saccharine sweet,
and Harpo Marx's death.
Media memories, great and small,
searing holes into our thoughts.
The worst generation, they called us all,
when the truth was all we sought.

A While Coming

I walked through
the garden full,
past rose petals
holding raindrops captive.
The green grass
holds its secrets
under its seemingly
quilted, layered top.
I drank from
a running brook
of crystal, azure,
icy cold water.
I took refuge
in the shade
of stoic trees,
ancient and understanding.
Laid supine, gazing
at a moonlit
black velvet tapestry
adorned with stars.
I felt home—
I felt centered—
I felt . . . peace.
A while coming.

-S. A. Gerber-

Asylum

A chance to awaken
and see life anew.
To drink from the cup
and feel freshly renewed.

To watch the rain fall
upon the green hills.
Nourishing the herds,
while washing away ills.

To witness buds blossom,
and birds that sing.
Bright, sunlit skies
and every little thing.

To be given asylum,
accepted at a glance.
Or granted the option
of a rare second chance.

Time Out

Days passing slowly
into night.
Helpless feeling of
dreaded repetition.
The dark fog will
not dissipate.
The clock has frozen.
Rain is on
the sundial.
Look past.
Look forward.
There is no now.
Where does the sand
go when the hourglass
is full?

~S. A. Gerber~

Sunshine of a Dream

Basking in the sunshine
of a dream.
Soaking up the last
of the unconscious.
Colors are all
as they should be.
All trespassers are warned
to keep distant.
Only the night is
invited to intrude.
The cool dark
meshes with reality.
The dream remains intact,
as it will.

Calm Redemption

Dark arrives
by way of cloud.
Covers our area
like a shroud.

Huddled together
on a rain-soaked day.
Glances speak volumes;
nothing to say.

Sharing warmth
in a tent quickly built.
Really nothing more
than a well-worn quilt.

Whispered desires
now the only sound.
Save for the rain
pelting the ground.

Passionate love
made under violent skies.
The final redemption,
the calm in your eyes.

-S. A. Gerber-

Escape

I saw a saint
slinging down on
the ocean front.
Saw the waves
recoil in anger.
I saw gulls
hovering high above,
circling something dead.
Saw dark clouds
envelop the west.
I tried to buy
coffee or whiskey.
No one took cash.
I smoked in defiance
of the law.
I attempted refuge
in a friend's room.
She left to meet
someone to save her.
From her window,
I saw the wretched
gather in the rain.
I swallowed something
to escape somewhere.

Tainted Souls

The postman delivers off the hour.
He leaves odd footprints, adding
upheaval to my garden.
All men of madness send me
letters daily seeking advice.
They live on electricity and hope
and found my name in old
and yellowing files.
They ask the same question over
and over again;
"How much does a tainted soul go
for on the street?"
They have lost their voices pleading
in vain for insane demands and have
lost their hearts to wanting.
They attempt to paint blue skies with
black ink and raise flowers in the sand.
They strain at leashes still held by masters
and howl at a misunderstood sun.
I cannot help them.
At present, the masters are cutting the
palm trees from my garden . . .
and counting the circles in my mind.

~S. A. Gerber~

Fare Thee Well

Bottled and bonded,
bought and sold.
Fear of living
is growing old.

Flaw in emotions
show straight through.
No chance now
of being true.

Life's loves lost
not easily said.
Shattered of soul,
better off dead.

I regret saying,
"Fare thee well."
Now Dante's circles
crowed as hell.

-S. A. Gerber-

Clouds

Grand cumulus clouds
speak solely to me.
I know their powers
and their subtleties.
They can dissipate
for the sunlight
or produce a jar full
of blessed rain.
With their magic, they
envelop me like a
soft, gray comforter,
casting down their
cool daytime darkness.
They are truly born again,
for there are new ones
every day.

On Borrowed Time

The lyrical muse
speaks to me
in such softness.

With her voice
of light rain
and indigo eyes.

In a whisper
she conveys dreams
not yet ventured.

Hair like platinum;
skin, electric fleece,
she glides unseen.

I can convince
no one of
her angelic presence.

Perhaps she is
only a dream . . .
on borrowed time.

~S. A. Gerber~

The Day is Long

Just a word,
what it's worth.
Will a prayer
save the earth?

In this life,
they do say,
"We must survive
yet another day."

After the moon,
blood red sun.
Predicts the world
will be undone.

To now repent,
would seem wrong
and dishonest as
the day is long.

Under the Radar   06/18/10

Under the radar
my sails blown down.
Under the radar
my time has grown.
Gain more freedom
from the gathered masses,
much less pursuit
to the ruling classes.
To write, pil gorge
how powerful the phenomenal.
To publish and be read
and still stay anonymous,
Solitude and recluse
go hand in hand.
I am still quite restless

Personal freedom diverge
like circles on water.
A wave of drama
breaks wash ashore.
art is pornographic;
the church too stingy
Islam is too violent;
not like the crusade.
Sunday wines are
nothing but ill gotten
gain ... unless donated.
Charities give receipts.

(see some lines
elsewhere)

Under the Radar

Under the radar,
my seeds are sown.
Under the radar,
my time is my own.

Far more freedom
from the masses.
Much less visible
to the ruling classes.

To write and purge,
pretty much synonymous.
Must publish and be read
and still stay anonymous.

Solitude and recluse
go hand in hand.
I'm quite content
leaving smaller prints in sand.

He who has chosen
to blow his own horn,
will reap what he deserves,
in ridicule and scorn.

I'm under the radar,
flying life low.
Under the radar,
living status quo.

Of Thee

Nose-diving like a
broken songbird into
the catgut net
of reality.

Losers form a line to
the right for a
second helping
of ignorance.

A parched, dying earth
is nourished only by
the sweat and urine
of wanderers.

Every day, students and graduates,
painters and poets die by
various means
of boredom.

The outcasts and the mad
leave bite marks and swallow
the huge bites they take
of life.

-S. A. Gerber-

Marbled Sunrise

Awoke to what I
call a "marbled
sky sunrise."
You know, those
colors and effects
you only see of
a desert morning.
It's about 0620ish.
No birds chirp;
too cold.
Full trees usually
blocking view
stand leafless.
Very few cars are
heard heading
to work.
Put on the coffee
and light the fireplace.
Going over notes
as the radio offers
up a bit of Bach
this morning.
Nothing comes from
my pen this early,
but I try.

My Muse prefers
to come by night.
The "girls" awake
from their special
cat spots to
enjoy breakfast.
After that and a
drink of water,
they return to sleep.
Sounds good, however,
I am usually not up this
early on a day off,
so, I'll continue
to try and put pen to
paper, mostly as an
excuse to enjoy the sunrise.
I've missed so many
in my life.

-S. A. Gerber-

Count the Stars

Standing in the rubble
of a sand castle ruin,
recalling the words
to a forgotten tune.

The razor fades dull
as gray clouds accumulate,
the wine almost gone
but still time to ruminate.

Gulls above circle noisily,
looking for a spot to land.
They do not seem to care to light,
on the rain-soaked sand.

Ole Mama Earth has exhausted
another gaping large yawn,
adding to the insignificance
that we are all just really pawns.

Up to pack for the sojourn on,
though not too close or too far.
Just another spot of similar peace
to lay back and count the stars.

New Day Sun

The sky above,
unfolds its blue.
The ground takes
on another hue.
Bird in flight,
takes its time.
One with all,
reason and rhyme.
The ocean roars
its mighty sound,
taking ships and
all it found.
Mountains stand stoic
through it all,
never to crumble,
never to fall.
Tree limbs rattle
in the wind,
trembling meekly as
though they sinned.
Blue sky darkens,
as if done,
only until tomorrow's
new day sun.

~S. A. Gerber~

Confession

Never did hang much with
the guys who worked on engines,
the guys who could fix things.
Remember in high school, a guy
would pull up in a hot rod,
open the hood, and the tech terms
would start to fly?

"Four barrel,"
"Offenhauser intake,"
"Jack shaft,"
"Glass packs,"
"Headers."

Got to confess, I never knew what
the dickens they were talking about.
There was never any inherent dislike.
Some of them were friends,
just with different common ground.
None of them then would have known:

Tennessee Williams,
Steinbeck,
Byron or Shelley,
Kubrick,
Polanski.

That's okay.
Guess it all evens out in the end.
One of those guys is now some big
NASCAR owner.
Another is a vice president of world-
wide something for Prudential.
And here I sit scribbling this crummy
poem.

Bullies

They were always a
few years older, the
schoolyard and park
bullies.
Always bigger, stupider,
always fronting for
someone.
I tended to defend myself
with verbal wit, which
to these guys, was more
confusing than fists.
I generally got the worst
anyway.
I understand them now
after Psych. I & II.
In an off-campus saloon,
over strong drink the
professor pointed out a new
breed.
You know, the "ineffectual" . . .
oops, pardon me . . . the
"**intellectual**" bully.
You know, the guy in class
or coffeehouse who read
some Schopenhauer or
Spangler and has all the
answers.

-S. A. Gerber-

Constantly interrupts, listens,
but does not hear.
Talks, but says nothing.
After suffering these types of
boors, I wonder now how the
schoolyard and park variety
made it through life.
You can't intimidate everyone
forever.
Wonder if they are even still
around.
I know for a fact the "**ineffectuals**"
are.

Covers

"Maybe the same entity appeared
different to different masses", he said.
"They just saw Him as He wanted to
be seen. Maybe that's how the same
story got so widespread back then."

Pretty insightful.

Just goes to show about books and their covers.
Most just write him off as a big oafish-
looking boob with a Southern accent.
This is not the case.
He just may possess a touch of the poet.
Thankfully, I never go by popular opinion.
I would miss out on many of the "rough
diamonds" that orbit my world.
Calling at all hours and sitting in my
living room until dawn, attempting to put
the world right by way of word and deed.
This guy has a clear perspective on reality.
He not only laughed, but heartily agreed
that a hundred monkeys with a hundred
typewriters, would eventually compose
The Lord's Prayer.

Remember about covers.

The original cover to *Catcher in the Rye*
was nothing to look at either.

-S. A. Gerber-

Twelve in '66

A '66 fastback,
candy-apple red.
The Beatles' *Revolver*,
"She Said She Said."

Sixth-grade graduation,
a girlfriend bond.
First heard Dylan's,
Blonde on Blonde.

One year away,
from the Summer of Love.
Sgt. Pepper's and 'Frisco,
Hawks and Doves.

LBJ and RTD,
IRS and NAACP,
PLO and JDL,
USA and LSD.

Vietnam and campus unrest
stirred up quite a mix.
But I could only sit and watch,
I was twelve in '66.

Dire Circus

Wagons roll in,
set up stage.
Book of life,
add a page.

The dire circus
sets up camp.
Fresh straw under
an oil lamp.

The beat animals
in silent parade.
The ringmaster drinking
in the shade.

Clowns stand knowing
all the while,
nothing they do
generates a smile.

All in all,
no one comes.
Just empty bottles
left by bums.

Pull up stakes
without a sound.
Head for another
long-dead town.

~S. A. Gerber~

Elsewhere

Heavy traffic is increasing;
I see it in my living room.
Thunder continues to roll, so I
can't keep my mind on my papers.
Exploding cars and people land
standing upright on my front lawn.
I would get up to dance, but the
music is not right.
In a dark closet in back, someone
paints an eerie self-portrait.
The gathered drink plenty, however,
they lack the real thirst of genius.
I can no longer pretend life.
The ceiling of the farm is erupting,
and I long for quiet elsewhere.
Ships sail and trains roll every day,
and somewhere, there are twenty-five
acres waiting in my mind.

Bleak Witness

I see the sidewalks sweat
and the stucco swelling.
The streets fill with
groups of parasitic voyeurs.
All want a taste of death
without really dying.
A harsh, burning light invades
the comforting darkness.
The guilty scatter like
oiled drops of mercury.
Presently, the sky takes on
a particular look of sadness.
Birds fall from branches in a
way that defies known nature.
A distant dirge can be heard
over the plaintive wail of a child.
I bear bleak witness to an ancient,
foretold maze of myths.
Cannot say which myth was correct.
There is such familiarity to them all.

-S. A. Gerber-

Morning Cries

Morning cries bitterly against the
dark revenge of night.
The unforgiving sidewalks and
back alleys teem with life.
Moon saints and sinners stand
poised with sharpened wits, looking
for an eternal battle to win.
The roar of buses adds to the
sweet fumes of the city inhaled
by nine-to-fivers in silhouette against
an electrically charged backdrop.
Cheap neon and dim bulbs emanate
from greasy, old establishments
crowded with the hot breath of wanting.
Humid air clinging to bodies like
used cooking oil make for the sweet-
sour smell of self-solitude.
Dawn rising like an intrusion is the
enemy of all that is sacred in the night.
Hot blood and chilled reason sing
a disturbing mantra along the halls of
soon-to-be decayed saloons.
Knowledge comes to those who wait—
Nothing can survive the reality
of light.

Dream State

Sunshine blasts through
my open blinds.
Still in that
glorious dream state.
Phones are ringing,
doors are knocking.
Ignore it all.
My precious time
is my own.
My pen to
coffee-stained paper.
Don't need a
drink—
Don't need a
smoke—
Just need to
remain in the
glorious dream state.
Eventually I allow
reality an entrance;
and, I fear,
much too soon.

-S. A. Gerber-

Washington Dream

I woke up naked in
the Space Needle;
I was escorted out
in post and in haste.
Ate my breakfast in
the kitchen of a
lawyer friend's wife;
hung-over like hell
in borrowed clothes.
I wrote poetry at Fourth
and Pike and read it at
the Hurricane Café.
At First and Pike, I drank
coffee in a subversive
bookstore across from
the big market; later,
I puked into the Sound.
Prowled misty streets
by night in search of
a Mexican restaurant;
stumbled into Mama's
Kitchen for beer and beans.
I listened to guitar music
in a downtown plaza and
was reminded of the Bay
Area, circa '67-'68.
I awoke in a moody drizzle
and looked for a room
to retire to.

Literary Wish List

I want to drink like Faulkner,
write like Fitzgerald,
and go out like Hemingway,
with a blast, double-barreled.
Have passion like Capote
or a hard ass like Mailer.
I think of Hart Crane,
courting a drunken sailor.
I want to soak up life
like dear old St. Jack
returning always to the womb
of stately Mother Kerouac.
I want mythic recluse,
like Pynchon and Salinger,
safe in the assumption
there will never be a challenger.

~S. A. Gerber~

Some Simple Wants

I want to:

Live by my own hours/rules.
Watch my tomatoes and eggplants grow.
Burn my uniforms.
Own and operate a bookstore/coffee joint.
Infect the city with my own madness.
Throw a pie at Miss America.
Have grilled cheese and fries at 3 a.m.

I want to:

Have all animals/friends live forever.
Drink with Edgar Allan Poe in the afterlife.
Date Mary Shelley there too.
Speed through the universe with a Native-
American psychedelic guide.
Read Ginsberg in court, and
Henry Miller in the schoolyard.

I want to:

Dance naked into the clear light and
howl at the moon.
Roar into the Valley of Megiddo, and
make love in the library.
I want assurance of a higher power
and a wolf-shepherd hybrid pup.

I also want:

All nations to disarm.
No conflicts of any kind.
One world peace.

I'll probably live to see and attain all
except the last three.

Can't win them all.

-S. A. Gerber-

My Country

America, my country.

Once a beautiful countenance,
now tarnished with a scowl
of hatred.
Honesty and integrity in business,
now replaced by cunning, cons,
and craft.
The streets teem with folks bearing
hollow eyes and vapid smiles.
Long-established newspapers go
the way of buggy whips, as reality
television flourishes.

America, my country.
Someone pulled a fast one.

The turgid eight years of the last
administration has set back the cause
of reform for untold decades to come.
The Bush-Man has grown fat.
No voices of dissent have been produced.
Where is Mark Rudd?
Huey?
Bobby?
Ministers King and Malcolm?
Where is Bobby Zimmerman of Hibbing?
Where is Tom Hayden even? My former
city councilman.
George and Dick have fostered and heartily
embraced a culture of vacancy, ignorance,
and abeyance.

America, my country.

She has suffered permanent scars as disfiguring
as pockmarks on a fashion model.
At her present age and state of being, recovery
will be slow and painful.
I fear never will come the day when her smile
will reach from sea to shining . . . whatever.
The damage is done in the eyes of others, and again,
I fear that it may be indelible.

America, my country.

Strive to restore your former beauty.
A fine standing and a bright light
among the global community.
Reinstate your former status in
accountability and trust.
Be the model for all nations as once
was the case.
Make your children proud.
And even more difficult,
make an optimist of me.

-S. A. Gerber-

We Are

We are the 99 percent,
the ones who manufacture the peanuts
and get paid with the shells.
We are the condescended to,
the lied to,
the cheated,
the appeased,
the expendable.
We are young Mr. Lincoln and Emmett Till.
We are Medgar, Bobby, Dr. King, Jack,
and Minister Malcolm.
We are four dead girls on a Birmingham Sunday
and four dead students on an Ohio campus.
We are Daniel Ellsberg and Deep Throat.
We are Nixon's enemies list.
Berkeley Free Speech and Save the Whales.
We are Dan Rather and Cronkite,
PBS and NPR.
We are Lenny Bruce and Pryor,
Kesey and Kerouac,
Salinger and Richard Wright.
We are Randle P. McMurphy and Bigger Thomas.
We are the Hollywood Ten and the Chicago Seven.
We are Watergate and Vietnam.
We are this and that.
We are in Oakland; we are, finally, Scott Olsen.
We are sick and tired of the corporate greed,
betrayal, backstabbing.
Sick of the lies and the

cheating and of shouldering the burden while
the rich get richer.
Sick to the death of the insensitivity of corporations,
health care, and government acting without
conscience or restraint.
We are here!
We are ready!
We will not be out of your thoughts.
We will occupy every city.
Whether it gets Altamont or Woodstock
is entirely its choice.
Unfortunately, even the rules of how the game is played
resides with the ruling class; this, too, shall pass.

-S. A. Gerber-

Cash In

They make out
like the fat rats
they are and
still have the vanity
to fear death more
than the rest.
Velvet-cushioned
silver-spooned
country-club life
must be as hard to
relinquish as nicotine.
CEOs, CFOs
War-and-whore-
mongers alike
want to cling
to their chips
until the end.
To be the
last to cash in.
Seems like the
least deserving
want to survive
the most . . .
at any cost.

Kudos to the
Jukebox-listening
Beer-guzzling brethren.
The factory and machine
workers. The
dirty-nailed laboring
unwashed.
They have cashed in.
They don't hoard
or stockpile.
They never whine
about death.
Don't have time . . .
they don't fear it.
Do you?

-S. A. Gerber-

Desperation

Letting go of what is
left of the Golden Rule.
Anyone remember ethics?
Kierkegaard . . ? . . Kant . . ?
Neither can I.
As angry sea birds swoop
down to pick at bones
left bleached in the sun;
some attempt to re-raise
a tattered emblem in hopes
of emboldening those who
were once soldiers to battle.
The fight once put to rest
now seems worthwhile again.
Always does to those who hold
the shares and the interest;
never the weapons.
The most popular deity by
majority rule and desperation
stands on their side as they
swallow up cultures like
so much plankton.
Imposing the will of right
by gunpoint.
How hard they push and fight
against this fragile little world . . .
third from the sun and light-years,
from what I feel, was really intended.

Midterms

Tuesday, November 2, 2010:
Midterm Election Day.

I still think this is a waste as I wait
in line at my polling place.
I barely got to finish the H. S. Thompson bio
I was reading before Larry came a' knocking.
He insisted that I come exercise my right or
I would regret it as he had done for not voting last time.
So now, wired up on coffee in yesterday's clothes,
here I stand.
We'll probably just cancel each other out,
Larry and I, but I see a lot of kids who don't
even look eighteen waiting to cast ballots.
Kids are rarely conservative and generally vote
on the side of the angels.
I try to keep that hope going as I
watch the returns later on MSNBC.
Pretty depressing, but hey, I said
it would probably be a waste.
History can bear me out.
After all, any populace who elected
Nixon, Reagan, and George Jr.
in twice pretty much gets what it deserves.

Tallis Qualis.

-S. A. Gerber-

All That Whiskey

I finish your drink
on the nightstand
as I listen to you
in the shower.
The sound of the
running water puts
my brain at ease
in this den of empty
bottles and vacant hearts.
Just another night,
a replay of déjà vu,
to coin a redundancy.
I should be happier tonight;
the place is paid for the
month, and the fridge is full.
But more importantly,
I almost got the words out.
Almost said it this night.
Damn close.
All that whiskey.
It loosens the inhibitions,
but drowns the emotions.
I find this really irritating
until I remember that
that's the reason I drink in
the first place.

~S. A. Gerber~

Elemental Aggression

The wind is hitting
like a sledgehammer,
the likes of which
not witnessed in years.
I'm inside with Coltrane
and reading F. Scott Fitz.
The kind of wind
Mr. Baum wrote about,
the kind that lands
you in Oz.
Dangerous, annoying, and
unpredictable is wind.
The foulest of all elements.
Better the snow
turned to slush,
the spark to flame,
the rain to flood.
Blowing harder now.
Some demon is
feeding its intensity.
The sound now drowns
out all else,
an aggressive, mean sound,
indifferent, insensitive, untamed.
Whoosh whash schoo!
So much for onomatopoeia.
I just lost power.
I finish this and the night by candlelight.
Look for it over the rainbow.

Nowhere Special

Off the road
to nowhere
special.
Untied and
unfettered.
Finding exhilaration in:

The diners,
the gas stations,
the dollar stores
(talk about inflation;
they used to be dime stores),
the libraries,
the newsstands,
the drugstores.

How magical it is to
pull into a small-town
carnival right at sunset.
How removed and innocent
the child looks on the front
yard tire swing of early morn.

These images seem almost
otherworldly, yet here
they stand, for the present,
uncorrupted by the surrounding
big cities.

They still exist in hidden
pockets, off the beaten track.
Seek them out before they
exist only in faded memory.

-S. A. Gerber-

Intrude

In the dark,
the comfort comes.
In the night,
the starlight hums.

Broken glass lies
on the ground.
A lost wish
is never found.

The waves break
upon the shore.
The land erodes
more and more.

When will dawn
intrude the dark,
which will forever
leave its mark?

Wish You Were Here

(June 6, 1944-June 6, 2010)

The "greatest invasion," D-Day,
was sixty-six years ago today.

My pop was there—3rd Armored
Division—Omaha Beach.

He also made the Battle of the Bulge.
He said it was a rotten winter in Belgium.

After all that, it was cancer that killed
him at sixty-six, thirty-eight years after D-Day.

He was there,
but he's not here.

War is hell . . .
so is life.

-S. A. Gerber-

Burn the Flowers

Gather the rain.
Store it away.
May be needed
some other day.
Stand a ground
over the grave.
Fresh, new mound
just been made.
Burn the flowers
in the flame.
Smell the ashes
just the same.
Lounge back supine.
Wonder at stars.
Look to tomorrow
to nurse scars.

Service

They sing their
song of daytime—
these fellow travelers.

Well-insulated in
their own vehicle—
very much alone.

Buffered by coffee
and a smoke—
on their way.

A cold morning
a gray day—
rain to come.

Also alone in
thought and action—
no sideways glances.

Fighting their way
the same everyday—
to serve someone.

The Blank Page

Sitting at the keyboard,
facing the blank page.

Outside my window . . .
a party on the next block.

Sounds of glass breaking,
drunken laughter,
guys belching,
girls squealing,
water splashing,
gun shots . . .
sirens.

Sitting at the keyboard,
facing the blank page.

Some people have all the fun.

~S. A. Gerber~

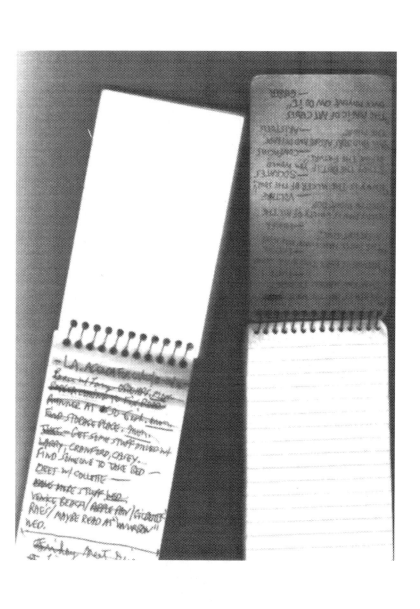

Whirlwind

Last-minute decision (left up to my wifey)—
LA for Thanksgiving!
A whirlwind tour.
Budget tighter than a rabbi's wife.
No rental car.
Taking wifey's.
Gas money only, with few exceptions:
Pocket change for coffee at Dutton's (no books!)
and twenty for the poker game.
(If I get fat there, maybe Hollywood Park.)
We will eat courtesy of friends and relatives,
Stay gratis at Mumsey's, and my wifey has
vowed not to make a purchase on Black Friday.
No Jazz Bakery with Tom & Crawford
or even lunch on the pier.
Maybe a midnight bus ride to downtown
to hang among the fellow destitute.
Spend the night drinking wine in the gutter
and writing poetry no one will hear.
No worries about being hit up for change.
Anyone there will have more on them than I will.
Ride the bus back in the morning hours,
disappointed and sober, even though I will swear
I saw the ghost of *Chinaski among the ruins.
Renewed or not, back on the road come Saturday.
Back to the reclusive mind state I call home.

*Charles Bukowski

Test

Been in the ol' Barnes & Noble café
for an hour and a half now.
Came from a semi-interview,
so I'm dressed semiprofessional;
khakis, sneakers, shirt, and "Dead" tie.
Spent my last two bucks on coffee.
Finished up my application.
Went through City Life,
deciding to buy the Capote bio.
Don't know anyone here today;
no Hank,
no Mickie,
no Bob or Bullington.
I have a 527-question psych test to complete.
Ha!
One look at this, and the semi-company
will scramble to set new standards!
I will be determined and judged as
some kind of mutant.
They will sell it to Harvard
to be used as standard text,
for weeding out the truly mad.
It will be the Rosetta Stone by which all
future miscreant applicants will be measured.
They'll want me after I'm dead to put in
a jar and be studied.
Even if I have a job by then,
I'll quit for that kind of honor.

The Season

Having some of what Lenny Bruce
called Jewish marijuana—tea *mit* lemon.
A little winded now.
Had to trudge up to the executive
offices for the lemon.
Just squirt it into my hot, herbal
mixture and I should be on
the mend in no time.
The flu kills some thousands of
people each year, ya' know.
Mostly *older* people yet.
Getting ahead of myself here.
I don't even know if I have the flu.
Could be sinuses or allergies;
I shouldn't have come in today.
Can I take Coricidin with tea?
Will it react badly? Give me the fear?
Calm yourself, Gerb, my boy, calm yourself.
I'm a guy who used to swallow anything
that had initials with cheap whiskey.
Now I'm worried about tea and cold medicine!
So goes the season.
The cold and flu season.
I missed the last two that went around.
This is payback—times two.

~S. A. Gerber~

Alternative

The terrifying feeling
of oncoming madness
cannot be battled!
Something else is in control.
Inside your head, it feels
like the fast flickering
of a light switch, on and off.
A lost feeling of disassociation
from the rest of the body ensues.
A helpless sensation of just
having landed as a stranger
to this world.
A quick electrical surge through
the mind every minute or so.
Total impatience with anyone
attempting to communicate.
An icy wave of both victimization
and alienation hitting at once.
An all-out case of . . . "The Fear."

This is all from withdrawal from
an anti-anxiety pill! Supposed to help!
Some great alternative to the last
one I took. All prescription, yet!
I don't remember street drugs
treating me this badly.

On Twenty-five Years

(04/18/85—04/18/10)

It's April eighteenth,
and I just wanna' say,
in a manner of speaking,
today's my birthday!
Yep, sober and clean
for twenty-five years.
No whiskey, no drugs,
not even some beers.
Quite a long path
to clarity's door, though
you'd all be on your knees,
if you knew me before.
But I followed the road
down a well-worn line.
Even if the early years,
were ten minutes at a time.
So, if I can make twenty-five,
there is hope and life for any.
For now I'm alive with the few,
instead of dead with the many.

The Quotable Gerb

(Thus Far)

"I'm too old, to die young."

"Never sell your soul---- lease it."

"A rough walk makes for a sweet rest."

"I'll find a great method for suicide,
even if it kills me."

"Not gambling is a great system."

"Art loses its magic once anyone can do it."

"Stage acting is life----times two."

"If you're a drunk, the glass better be half empty."

"Fanatic fundamentalist religion is more dangerous
than are bombs, guns, and women."

"You can never have enough excess."

"Be yourself----no one's watching anyway."

"No one worth cultivating calls during the day."

"If any of my stuff has depressed you, then you understand."

"If my stuff garners praise **after** I'm dead, it'll serve me right."

"No great work of art is born of happiness."

Exchange

I'd trade all friends
for one good dog.

Trade all burglar alarms
for a decent twelve gauge.

A house in a good neighborhood
for a shack on twenty-five acres.

I'd trade a fifty inch plasma
for a great library.

All the politicians
for one honest plan.

Trade a beamer
for a Harley.

I would trade the wind
for the rain, and---

this life---
for immortality.

S. A. Gerber is a native of Los Angeles, California, who currently resides in Las Vegas, Nevada. He has been writing for decades and has had several readings of his stage plays, but nothing as yet produced. The same luck has also met his screenplays and scripts for television thus far. (He could, however, wallpaper his office with all the positive rejections he has garnered). He came to settle on poetry because it uses less paper.

S. A. Gerber's poetry has been published in such diverse magazines as, *Desert Voices* and the *Blue Collar Review*. He is also working on a novel . . . his first . . . and plans to release several more volumes of poetry this year. For paychecks, in the past, he has worked in Film, Video, Fundraising and Security.

He and his lovely wife and their host of animals hope to move back to Los Angeles next year, should the Mayas be wrong about 2012.

Notes

Notes

Doodles

Doodles

Phone Numbers

Phone Numbers